THE AMENDMENT

OF THE

FEDERAL CONSTITUTION.

AN ADDRESS

BEFORE THE

Christian Association for National Reformation,

OF SOUTHERN ILLINOIS,

BY REV. JAMES WALLACE,

IN REV. S. WYLIE'S CHURCH, EDEN,

November 8, 1864.

ADOPTED UNANIMOUSLY, AND ORDERED TO BE PUBLISHED.

ST. LOUIS:

GEORGE KNAPP & CO., PRINTERS AND BINDERS.

1865.

THE AMENDMENT

OF THE

FEDERAL CONSTITUTION.

AN ADDRESS

BEFORE THE

Christian Association for National Reformation,

OF SOUTHERN ILLINOIS,

BY REV. JAMES WALLACE,

IN REV. S. WYLIE'S CHURCH, EDEN,

November 8, 1864.

ADOPTED UNANIMOUSLY, AND ORDERED TO BE PUBLISHED.

ST. LOUIS:
GEORGE KNAPP & CO., PRINTERS AND BINDERS.
1865.

THE AMENDMENT OF THE FEDERAL CONSTITUTION:

AN ADDRESS*

Before the Christian Association for National Reformation, of Southern Illinois,

BY REV. JAMES WALLACE,

In Rev. S. Wylie's Church, Eden, November the 8th, 1864.

Adopted unanimously, and ordered to be published.

Mr. President—Ladies and Gentlemen:

The duty of nations to acknowledge the true God, and submit themselves to Jesus Christ as their Lawgiver and King, is of the highest importance, and underlies all moral and political questions. The moral character of a nation—its continued existence and prosperity—and the character and happiness of its people—depend, largely, upon the relation which it sustains to God, and the obedience which it renders to his law. It is not a question of political economy, or banks, or tariff, or war, or peace, we enter upon, but one underlying all these, and giving to them their value and importance.

This subject commends itself to the heart of every true christian. The authority of the Lord Jesus Christ over his own people, in all their relations and interests, and entire obedience to him, is accepted by every christian as the first duty he owes to his Lord and Saviour, and is essential to christian character, and to all spiritual enjoyment and progress in the divine life. "Lord, what wilt thou have me to do?" "If ye love me," says Christ, "keep my commandments." "Ye are my friends if ye do whatsoever I command you."

And this principle of entire and universal obedience to Jesus Christ—which is the foundation of christian character and happiness, and binds together in one blessed brotherhood all the children of God on earth—every true christian desires to see extended over all the world, till all men and nations shall submit themselves to Emanuel as Lord of all. And it is not easy to understand how an individual who has accepted Jesus Christ as his only Lord and King, and solemnly promised obedience to him in all things, can oppose the nation (of which he forms a part) acknowledging the same authority, and submitting itself to him as King of kings and Lord of lords. That such

---

* By appointment at the previous meeting.

opposition exists on the part of infidels, and the known enemies of the Redeemer, is not to be wondered at; but that any professed christians should unite with them in refusing to have this Man reign over them in their civil relations, is as strange as it is lamentable; and can be found only in minds still ignorant of the character and claims of the exalted Messiah as Governor among the nations, and under the influence of inveterate prejudice and sectarian bigotry.

As the acknowledgment of God as the Creator of all things does not entitle a man to be regarded as a christian—infidels do so,—so the acknowledgment of God in his essential character by a nation, does not entitle it to be regarded as a christian nation. In this character God has no dealings with men or nations, and they can have no dealings with him. All transactions between God and fallen man must be conducted upon the ground of the mediatorial economy, over which Jesus Christ is the constituted head. In his essential character, as apart from the person and work of Jesus Christ, the Mediator between God and man, God will receive no service or homage from persons or nations, and will bestow no blessing upon them. God has commanded all men to honor the Son even as they honor the Father; and he that honoreth not the Son, honoreth not the Father. The person or nation, therefore, that does not honor Jesus Christ, does not honor God. This truth is implied in all the revelation which God has given of himself in his Word, and the knowledge of it is necessary to all acceptable obedience and worship of God.

As the confession of Jesus Christ and professed subjection to him is necessary to constitute the christian character of a person, so the acknowledgment of Jesus Christ and professed subjection to him is necessary to constitute the christian character of a nation. The christian character of both persons and nations is judged and determined by professed and consistent subjection to the character and law of Jesus Christ as contained in the Word of God.

Some admit that the Federal Constitution should be so amended as to acknowledge the existence of God, but without any reference to Jesus Christ. They are willing to have the God of the Deist recognized in the Constitution, but they are not willing that the nation should acknowledge the Christian's God. Such an amendment would be of little practical use; it would only be a change from national Atheism to Deism. It would not give to the government a christian character. It is not such a change as the Word of God and the faith of his people demand. It would not save the nation from the threatenings of Divine wrath, pronounced against all nations that refuse to honor the Son, whom the Father hath commanded all men and nations to honor and obey. For the Eternal Father, from his throne in the heavens, has declared that all honor and obedience rendered to him must be given to his Son Jesus Christ, whom he has appointed Lord and Ruler of heaven and earth; and he commands all civil rulers to respect this divine appointment, and threatens certain and utter destruction upon all nations that reject or ignore Jesus Christ the King of nations. And lest any should imagine that nations are not bound in their corporate capacity to treat with and acknowledge Jesus Christ, God the Father expressly addresses civil rulers in their official character, and commands them to submit to the exalted Messiah as their Lawgiver and Ruler, and in case of refusal he threatens them with speedy and entire destruction. "Be wise now therefore, O ye kings; be instructed, ye judges of the earth. Kiss the Son, lest he be angry, and ye perish from the way, when his wrath is kindled but a little." And the Apostle Peter, quoting this psalm in the 4th chapter of the Acts, and charging the great sin of rejecting the person and authority of the Messiah upon the rulers of his day, both Jews and Gentiles, proves that the duties commanded in this psalm are not limited to any time or nation, but are universally binding at all times and upon all nations.

Here, then, we are clearly taught, that all nations to which the word of God comes, are distinctly and positively commanded by God to make a full and formal acknowledgment of Jesus Christ as their King and Lawgiver, and to receive and own him as their Lord and Ruler by a public national act of reverence, love, submission and adoration. This they must do as the only way of appeasing the wrath of heaven, and escaping the terrible strokes of the iron rod of the Lord's Anointed, by which he will dash in pieces, like a potter's vessel, all rulers and nations who ignore or oppose his universal dominion. Nations may and do commit other sins, and expose themselves to the temporary and wasting judgments of God; but ignoring or rejecting the authority of the Lord Jesus Christ, the King of kings and the Lord of lords, *first and most provokes* the wrath of God, and brings upon them speedy and utter destruction. All nations guilty of this sin must repent or perish—perish from the way, when the wrath of the Son of God "is kindled but a little."

True, God is merciful and long-suffering with guilty men and nations. He waits to be gracious; he gives time for repentance; he calls and he warns; he threatens, and he inflicts judgments, sometimes great and terrible, all in order to bring to repentance. But, if these are not heeded, the day of righteous and final retribution will surely come.

Here we might rest the argument. Why should the christian desire any further testimony? The will of God, clearly declared in his Word, is with him decisive and final. From it there is no appeal. We ought to obey God rather than men. But "God speaks once, yea, twice, but man perceiveth it not." He condescends to give "line upon line, and precept upon precept."

The same truth appears in the institution and nature of civil government. Civil rule is the ordinance of God. It is not a device of human wisdom, or an invention of men. Its origin is not to be found in the social compact, but in the will of God, made known by the light of nature, and more clearly revealed in the Bible. The powers that be are ordained of God. Civil rulers are God's ministers for good to the people. And like all other ordinances, human and divine, it must be administered according to the delared will of its Author. The great higher law of civil government is subjection to the exalted Mediator. God the Father commands it; Jesus Christ claims it; all holy angels and saints in heaven and on earth joyfully approve of it. None but devils, and wicked men (who are rebels against the divine government), oppose it. Civil rulers being God's servants are under special obligations to submit to this divine and beneficent arrangement. The official position and character of civil rulers, so far from exempting them from obedience to God's law, is the ground and reason of their obligation to obey it. While the Apostle Paul commands christians to be subject to the powers that be, he places the whole obligation of christians to obey civil rulers upon the ground of the relation which they sustain to God and the blessings which flow from the relation thus divinely constituted. They are God's ministers; he is the minister of God to them for good. Because civil rulers are the servants of God, christians should obey them. Civil rulers are clothed with the authority of God. They act in his name; they execute their office according to his law; they are God's deputies on earth. Obedience to them is obedience to God; resistance to them is rebellion against God. "Whosoever therefore resisteth the power, resisteth the ordinance of God; and they that resist" civil government thus constituted and administered, "shall receive to themselves damnation." (Rom. 13: 2.)

Thus it plainly appears that the whole claim of civil rulers upon the respect and obedience of the people, depends upon the relation which they sustain to God, as his appointed and approved servants. True, the people have a right to choose who shall rule over them: but the people are not the original source of power; for there is no power but of God. In the formation of their constitutions, and in the choice of their rulers, the people are under law to God. God alone is Lord of the conscience; and the enlightened conscience is responsive to the authority of God alone. The deep and universal conviction in our moral nature, that all power is of God, is the strong and broad foundation on which the stability and permanence of civil government rests in all nations. A government may for a time obtain the support of the people upon the narrow ground of expediency and policy; but if it has not a moral character corresponding with the laws of God, as his institution, it has no security for permanent existence.

The constitution of a government is a public declaration of the principles by which it is desirous to be known and judged by the inhabitants of its own territory and other nations. It contains the fundamental principles on which it demands the support and obedience of its own people and the respect of foreign powers. Now if there be in that constitution no distinct recognition of the character and authority of Jehovah, the source of all power, and of Jesus Christ, by whom kings reign and princes decree justice, and whom God has commanded all nations to hear and obey, there is wanting one of the primary elements of moral character and influence which goes to constitute the strength and stability of the nation; for such a constitution does not reach to the deep and innate principles of man's moral nature, which is the only sure and permanent basis of civil rule among men.

In the year 1861 most of the Southern States seceded from the General Government of the United States. The great radical error which led them to take this course was, that the Constitution of the United States is only a compact between sovereign and independent States—that the Government of the United States is a mere partnership concern, from which any of the parties can withdraw at pleasure. As there is no acknowledgment of the authority and law of God in the constitution, they did not see that while they were casting off the government they were rebelling against the authority of God. As God is not in the constitution, they did not believe that they sinned against him when they rejected its authority. Had there been in the constitution a distinct avowal of the supreme authority of God as the great Lawgiver, and the universal obligation of his law upon all men and nations, who can tell how far this great moral principle thus set prominently and authoritatively before the minds of the whole people, might have restrained the Southern States from their folly and madness, and saved the nation from the wholesale waste of blood and treasure consequent upon the present terrible civil war!

Civil rulers being God's ministers, should acknowledge him; the minister or servant should acknowledge his master. Nothing can be plainer; and this principle is recognized and acted upon, by every one, in the affairs of every-day life. Honest men will have no dealings with a servant who does not acknowledge his master or employer. Every man who enters upon office either civil or military, is expected to acknowledge the authority of him from whom his appointment comes; and failing in this, neither citizens nor soldiers will recognize his official character. And if it be necessary to have the lowest offices of civil and military power duly authenticated, to secure the respect and obedience of the people, how much more important in the highest and most responsible offices to which men are called! If the constable cannot enter the house of a citizen till he shows his authority, much more should the President, the Congress, or the Parliament, be able to show their authority before they assume to govern a nation. If the constable must acknowledge the magistrate before he can obtain a writ, much more should the rulers of a nation acknowledge the one Lawgiver before they make laws for the whole people. What would be thought of a man who, although duly elected by the people, would ignore the authority of the State? An insulted community would rise in their might and drive him from his official position; or, if this could not be done, every friend of good government and order would cease to acknowledge him as a lawful ruler. And if the man who would not acknowledge the authority of the State, which is minor and subordinate to the authority of God, would forfeit all claim to be regarded as a lawful ruler, in what light should men be viewed who disown and reject the authority of the Great Jehovah, the fountain of all authority and power? And if an intelligent and liberty-loving people would not submit to such usurpation, much less can it be supposed that the righteous moral Governor of nations, who is more jealous of his honor than men are of their freedom, will suffer his authority and law to be disowned and dishonored with impunity. If the Government of the United States will not permit its authority to be ignored in the revolted States, but will prosecute the war to "the bitter end" for the suppression of the rebellion, much more will the Most High God, who ruleth in the kingdom of men, vindicate his authority, and execute wrath to the uttermost upon every nation that does not submit to his righteous and universal dominion.

The sum of the argument is this: God has commanded all nations and their rulers to acknowledge Jesus Christ his Son; and threatened utter and inevitable destruction upon those nations that do not submit to him. This command is moral in its nature, and, as we have seen, is addressed to all civil rulers in all places and at all times, and consequently is binding upon the rulers and people of the United States. None will say that this nation has ever yet obeyed this command. It follows, of course, that, if God be God, it must repent and perform this duty, or be destroyed. There can be no other way.

The same principle occupies a prominent place in the history of nations contained in the Bible. Indeed, if there is any one truth taught more plainly than another in the Word of God, it is the supremacy of God's authority over nations, and their obligation to acknowledge him and obey his law. The great sin of Pharaoh, king of Egypt, on account of which the terrible and desolating judgments of Heaven came upon that nation, till it became the basest of kingdoms, from which it has never recovered, is contained in this language of that proud tyrant: "Who is the Lord that I should obey his voice?" Pharaoh believed the doctrine that nations are not under obligations to acknowledge and obey God, and he paid the penalty of his folly.

From the beginning to the end of the Israelitish and Jewish commonwealths, the great duty taught them by God, at sundry times and divers manners, was the public and formal acknowledgment of him as their King and Lawgiver, and the necessity and advantages of obedience to his law, and the dreadful and wasting judgments that would fall upon them, if, in any case, or at any time, they would renounce or act inconsistently with that relation in which they stood to him. All God's dealings with Israel, all the prosperity that nation enjoyed, and all the calamities it suffered, are calculated and designed to teach all other nations, in all succeeding generations, that that nation is blessed whose God is Jehovah, and that that nation or kingdom that will not serve him shall perish.

It was the professed subjection of Israel to God and obedience to his law, that constituted the national and political greatness of that people, and gave to them a lofty pre-eminence over all the surrounding nations. And Moses commands Israel to maintain this honorable relation, and continue in obedience to the law of God in all future time, as the only way of preserving that eminent distinction and prosperity which they had obtained and enjoyed. "Keep, therefore, and do them: for this is your wisdom and your understanding in the sight of the nations, which shall hear all these statutes, and say, Surely this great nation is a wise and understanding people: for what nation is there so great, who hath God so nigh unto them, as is the Lord our God in all things that we call upon him for? And what nation is there so great, that hath statutes and judgments so righteous as all this law, which I set before you this day?" (Deut. 4: 6-8.)

The independence and prosperity of Israel, as a nation, always corresponded with their professed and practical subjection to the authority and law of God. When Israel served the Lord, their armies were irresistible and victorious over all their enemies, at home and abroad. And when they departed from the Lord, the Lord departed from them, and either civil war prevailed between the tribes, or some of the neighboring nations invaded their land, destroyed their cities and laid waste their country, or the armies of Israel became an easy prey to their more powerful foes and oppressors. "Thus the children of Israel were brought under at that time, and the children of Judah prevailed, because they relied upon the Lord God of their fathers." "For Pekah, the son of Remaliah, slew in Judah one hundred and twenty thousand in one day, which were all valiant men; because they had forsaken the Lord God of their fathers." (2 Chron. 13: 18, & 28: 6.) May not the fall of so many tens of thousands of valiant men in the present war, on so many battle fields, be accounted for in the same way?

The history of Israel and Judah is the proof and illustration of the duty of nations to acknowledge God and obey his law, and of the sin of ignoring and disregarding his authority and transgressing his law.

And the same truth occupies a prominent place in the history of other nations. The proud monarch of Babylon, looking down from his lofty palace upon the great metropolis of the world, and exulting in his superior wisdom and riches which he had displayed in building the grand and magnificent capital of his vast empire and of the world, was instantly dethroned and degraded to the condition of the beasts, and made to eat grass as oxen, until seven times passed over him, and he confessed that the Most High ruleth in the kingdom of men, and giveth it to whomsoever he will. And when this haughty despot had been sufficiently humbled, and confessed this truth, his understanding returned unto him, and he blessed the Most High, and praised and honored him that liveth forever and ever, whose dominion is an everlasting dominion, and his kingdom is from generation to generation. And all the inhabitants of the earth are as nothing; and he doeth according to his will in the army of heaven, and among the inhabitants of the earth, and none can stay his hand, or say unto him, what doest thou? And when this absolute and godless king had been thus humbled and repented of his political atheism, and confessed the universal supremacy of God over nations, and their duty to submit to his authority, he was prepared to receive again his crown and his sceptre. At the same time, says he, "My reason returned unto me; and, for the glory of my kingdom, mine honor and brightness returned unto me; and my counsellors and my lords sought unto me, and I was established in my kingdom, and excellent majesty was added unto me." (Dan. 4: 33-36.)

What christian does not earnestly desire, that all the ungodly despots of all nations were sent to the same school till seven times had passed over them, and they had learned to make the same humble, yet sublime confession! Such a school for the education of godless and infidel civil officers is one of the world's necessities, and the great desideratum of these times.

And the case of Nebuchadnezzar, the king of Babylon, is not an idle story written to please and amuse the readers of the Bible; but it is the illustration of a great moral law, binding upon all nations, to which all civil rulers and people would do well to give heed and obey. For the prophet Daniel told Belshazzar, the grand-son of Nebuchadnezzar, that all this had happened to his father; and because he knew it, and had not received the instruction it gave, therefore his kingdom is divided and given to the Medes. "And thou, his son, O Belshazzar, hast not humbled thine heart, though thou knewest all this. And the God in whose hand thy breath is, and whose are all thy ways, hast thou not glorified." "In that night was Belshazzar the king of the Chaldeans slain, and Darius the Median took the kingdom." Thus the powerful empire of Chaldea was destroyed for political atheism, and the remnants of its existence which have been dug out of the earth are monuments of the greatness and danger of its sin, and witnesses in behalf of the doctrine for which I plead.

Light shining from the pages of prophecy conducts us to the same conclusion. In the panoramic view given of the rise, character and fall of the great nations and empires of the world, as seen and described in prophetic vision, the doctrine of God's supremacy over all governments stands out in bold relief; and the great comprehensive and joyful truth which prophets have learned from the future, as inspired historians have from the past, is: The Lord reigneth. His kingdom ruleth over all. God is in prophecy as he is in history. And the entire destruction of great and powerful empires as described in prophecy, as well as their existing ruins, teach us, not only the authenticity of the divine prediction, but also that verily he is a God that judgeth in the earth. And the overthrow of the world powers of Assyria, Chaldea, Medo-Persia, Greece and Rome, for their impiety in usurping the high prerogatives of Him who is the only King and Potentate of the world, and in denying God who is above, are terrible demonstrations of the sin of national atheism and ungodliness. All these once powerful dynasties have been destroyed. Rome Papal will soon follow Rome Pagan, in order to make way for the universal kingdom of the Messiah; and that kingdom alone that is subject to his authority shall stand forever.

In the highest and brightest prospect of the happiness of this earth which prophecy presents before us, this great principle of Messiah's universal reign over the nations is the grand, fundamental and prominent truth which gives existence and character to those happy times. The great moral revolution in the nations of the world, by which they will change their ungodly and unchristian character, and acknowledge the universal dominion of Jesus Christ, and crown him Lord of all, will introduce the reign of righteousness, and peace, and joy, over all lands. And in view of this blessed and glorious event, all the inhabitants of heaven, anticipating the happy change in the state of the world, unite in a song of thanksgiving and praise unto God. "And the seventh angel sounded; and there were great voices in heaven, saying, The kingdoms of this world are become the kingdoms of our Lord, and of his Christ; and he shall reign forever and ever. And the four and twenty elders which sat before God on their seats, fell upon their faces, and worshipped God, saying, We give thee thanks, O Lord God Almighty, which art, and wast, and art to come; because thou hast taken to thee thy great power, and hast reigned." (Rev. 11: 15–17.)

And, again, in a farther and fuller display of millenial purity and happiness, when Jesus Christ appears in the glory and magnificence of his royal character as King of kings and Lord of lords; and, in his triumphant march over the earth, has destroyed all the great world powers that resisted his authority, and all nations have acknowledged him as the Prince of the kings of the earth, and realized the blessings of his universal and beneficent reign, the jubilant song of heaven rises higher, and all the inhabitants of the world, in obedience to the command from the throne of God, unite with holy angels and the myriads of the redeemed in the mansions of glory, in singing praise and thanksgiving to God. "And the four and twenty elders and the four beasts fell down and worshipped God, that sat on the throne, saying, Amen, Alleluia. And a voice came out of the throne, saying, Praise our God, all ye his servants, and ye that fear him, both small and great. And I heard as it were the voice of a great multitude, and as the voice of many waters, and as the voice of mighty thunderings, saying, Alleluia, for the Lord God omnipotent reigneth."

Thus the voice of inspired history and the voice of prophecy unite with the voice of

God, coming directly from his eternal throne in the heavens, commanding all nations to avouch him to be their God, and to obey his law. Those who will not believe this testimony, would not be persuaded though one rose from the dead.

The great end and design of God in instituting civil government on earth, was, to maintain the supremacy of his authority and law among men. And every government deserves to be regarded as the ordinance of God, or not his ordinance, as it is fitted in its constitution and administration to promote this end. But how can a government accomplish this end if its constitution ignores even the existence of God?

The cause of all the evils that exist in the world is rebellion against God, and the only cure for these evils is subjection to him. Jesus Christ has been appointed to declare the terms of acceptance to rebellious men and nations, and to receive from them the homage of loyal subjects. The terms are unconditional surrender, and submission to him as their Prince and Saviour.

Here is the great panacea for the world's sorrows. The leaves of this tree of life are for the healing of the nations; Jesus Christ is the only Saviour of nations as well as of persons; and to know and acknowledge him is necessary to national as well as personal salvation. The first commandment in God's law requires nations as well as individuals to acknowledge God to be the only true God and their God, and to worship and glorify him accordingly.

The acknowledgment of God and subjection to his law, we have said, is the only effectual cure for the evils that at present afflict the nations. For whatever partial or temporary changes for the better may be brought about in the moral state of society in regard to particular evils, no radical or permanent reformation can be effected until the rulers of the nations acknowledge God the source of all authority, and obey the only law of moral reform contained in his Word. Intelligent and entire subjection to Jesus Christ as Lord of all, is the great and only principle of personal, social, ecclesiastical and national reformation, as well as the only safe and permanent ground on which nations can stand.

But how far is the position which the governments of the nations occupy from this. "They know not, neither will they understand; they walk on in darkness; all the foundations of the earth are out of course." (Ps. 82: 5.) "The kings of the earth set themselves, and the rulers take counsel together against the Lord and against his anointed, saying, Let us break their bands asunder, and cast away their cords from us." (Ps. 2: 2, 3.) This is the standing stereotyped moral character of nations and their rulers at the present, as it has been in past times, drawn by the pen of inspiration.

But we are assured that this state of things will not last always. God will arise, judge the earth and inherit all nations. Jesus Christ will take to himself his great power and reign. All kings shall fall down before him, and all nations shall serve him. The kingdoms of this world shall become the kingdoms of our Lord and of his Christ. And the nation that first remembers and turns to the Lord, will inaugurate a grand moral revolution in the state of the world, and will be the harbinger of universal peace and joy and liberty to all people.

We earnestly desire to see the United States first in bringing the King back. And may we not hope that this republic, so highly favored of Heaven—among the last to take its place in the great family of nations—will be the first to bow before the throne of Emanuel; and that, penitent and purged of its great sins against God and man, it will take the lead in conducting the other nations into the possession of millenial happiness and glory, under the sceptre of the Lord of all; that, reformed and exalted to a high moral eminence, and exhibiting the great principles of civil and religious liberty on the largest scale, before the eyes of all peoples, it may be chosen and honored of God in the grand mission of levelling and moulding the nations of the world, and preparing them for the blessedness and glories of Messiah's millenial reign! As the American Declaration of Independence, asserting the inalienable rights of all men, caused the tyrannical thrones of Europe to tremble, so the American declaration of the sovereign rights and universal dominion of Jesus Christ, the Prince of the kings of the earth, will cause all the ungodly thrones of the world to totter and fall! So shall they fear the name of the Lord from the west, and his glory from the rising sun. Then the bright and joyful morning of millenial light and glory shall break upon the world. And the song of praise and joy begun by the Mississippi and the Hudson, will be taken up by the Thames, the Rhine, the Danube, the Ganges, and the Amazon, and will swell and roll in mighty peals over all lands, as the voice of many waters, and as the voice of mighty thunderings, till the earth shall ring again, in one harmonious, universal acclaim, "Alleluia! for the Lord God omnipotent reigneth!"

Here the highest aspirations of the christian and patriot unite. Here is the highest and brightest consummation of our fallen world!

Shall the Constitution of the United States be amended, so as to purge it of the great sins of infidelity and slavery, and assert the rights of all men, and acknowledge and submit to the authority of God and his law? Shall the nation become penitent for its great sins against God and man, and reform, and attain and enjoy happiness which many prophets and kings desired to see and might not? Shall it be the first-born of the nations, and enter upon and perform the grand mission for which it is singularly fitted and called of God? Or shall it continue impenitent, and, with a punishment corresponding with its superior privileges, follow the wake of desolation and destruction of those nations upon which the Almighty has poured out his wrath because they did not call upon his name?

These questions the christian people of this country are now called upon to consider and answer; and upon their answer depends the future existence, character and destiny of this republic.

The time when the Constitution of the United States was formed was very unfavorable for the organization of a christian civil government. Then Infidelity reigned in France with an almost absolute and uncontrolled sway. The voice of Christianity in that land was almost silenced, and was scarcely heard in public places. Infidel France is the name by which that nation is usually designated at that time. The Reign of Terror was then beginning. The strong tide of Atheism and Infidelity which soon after broke down all legal and constitutional barriers, and deluged that land in blood, was now rising to its height; and the friendly and intimate relations existing between France and this country, and the sympathy and help received in the war of the revolution, gave to French Infidelity great power and influence in the United States. Infidelity was then popular and fashionable in this country.

And, besides, the union of a dead church with the state, and the ghostly power of the Pope and Roman priesthood over the minds of the people in all the other nations of Europe; the oppression and degradation of the masses under the combined power of the king and priest, and the prostitution of Christianity in all the nations of the old world—all presented a forbidding and loathsome spectacle to the minds of the revolutionary patriots, and prejudiced them against the pure and benign religion of Christ, and led them to believe that a recognition of any of its fundamental principles was inconsistent with the liberties of the people. There was not at that time a government in Europe whose example could be safely followed. And these great men could see no middle ground on which civil government could set the sole of its foot between a corrupted and prostituted Christianity and Atheism: and they chose the latter. These considerations will help to account for the strange anomaly in the history of nations, of a government without a God! This is the strange and unsightly aspect in which the Federal Constitution presents this nation before the christian world and other nations; for the name of God is not in the constitution, nor is there any reference to Jesus Christ, or his law, or his providence. The little phrase "year of our Lord," at the end of the instrument, which might be found in any infidel document, will not satisfy any christian.

And this want of the name of God in the constitution was not a mere omission. The men who sat in that Convention were intelligent men, and they did what they meant to do. The disregard shown to God is the result of thought and design. At a time of great difficulty and danger in its sessions, when, on account of jarring opinions and interests, the prospect of forming a united government became almost hopeless, Dr. Franklin, though not a professor of religion, made a motion, that the future sessions of the Convention should be opened with prayer; and the motion, though not directly voted down, was shuffled and lost.* And Dr. Franklin, in a note in his published works, says, that except three or four persons, the Convention thought prayers unnecessary.

Even in the form of the oath of the President, where we would naturally look for the name of God, it is not found. The command of God is, "Thou shalt fear the Lord, and shalt swear by his name." This is the only lawful way of swearing. But the Convention thought it better to leave the form of the oath defective, than admit the name of God in the constitution. In excluding the name of God from the form of the oath, the command to swear by his name is disregarded; the ordinance is prepared, God is dishonored, and the President is permitted to substitute any creature, real or imaginary, in his place—all in order to keep the name of God out of the constitution.

Need it be thought strange that a Convention of such men, convened in circumstances and under influences so unfavorable, and acting in these ways, did not make any acknowledgment of God, or Jesus Christ, or his law; and did not form such a constitution as would have become the representatives of a christian nation?

No man who denies the Christian religion is thought to be inconsistent in swearing to support the Federal Constitution. The Atheist, the Deist, the Jew, the Mahometan and the Mormon, may take the prescribed oath to the constitution, and none of them is regarded as having acted inconsistently with his declared principles. This, beyond all question, proves that the constitution is not a christian document, and that whatever excellences it may possess, (and we cheerfully admit they are many,) it needs to be amended, so as to become the fundamental law of a christian republican government.

The people of this country are now loudly called upon in the providence of God, as well as in his Word, to rectify this wrong, to repent of this national sin, and to bring this government into professed and practical subjection to the Lord and his Anointed. The existence of the present civil war in this land, its gigantic proportions and its threatening aspects, and its continuance beyond the expectations of the wisest statesmen, clearly say, that God is now pleading a controversy with this nation. That slavery is the immediate or proximate cause of the war, can hardly be doubted by any whose eyes are open; and that God intends to destroy slavery by this war, is almost equally certain. The Lord is known by the judgment that he executeth. And that this nation is chargeable with another great sin in ignoring his character and authority as the Lawgiver and King of nations, needs no further proof; for he has in his providence labelled that sin upon the nation.

---

* See Madison's Papers, Vol. II., 984-6. See also Secret Debates and Proceedings of the Convention, p. 87, Albany, 1821.

And now he demands of this government to vindicate over rebels his authority as well as its own, and to assert his rights as well as the rights of the slave. And in the slow progress of the armies of the North in putting down this groundless and wicked rebellion, and in the many disasters that befall them, and in the tens of thousands who have already fallen upon many bloody battle fields—many of them the best men in the land, whose loss to the nation is irreparable—"the Lord's voice is now crying unto the city, and the men of wisdom shall see thy name: hear ye the rod, and who hath appointed it." (Micah, 6: 9.)

Shall the voice of God now speaking in his Word, and calling in tones of thunder in his providence to this nation to submit itself to his authority and to accept Jesus Christ as its Prince and Saviour, be heard and obeyed? *This is the question.* To this question only one answer can be given from every christian heart; for none of them will say they will not have this Man to reign over them. Whatever differences exist among christians of different names on other and minor points, they are all agreed that there is but one Lord. And so soon as the movement to bring the government of the United States to acknowledge their common Lord, and to submit to his authority is fully understood, it must secure the cordial approval and earnest co-operation of all true christians.

Ungodly civil government is the chief instrumentality by which the Devil has succeeded in dividing the church, and scattering the power of the holy people, for almost three thousand years. Questions growing out of corrupt and immoral systems of government have been the main cause of dividing the most orthodox and pure churches, in Europe and America, for the past two hundred years. National sins have produced ecclesiastical divisions. The rejection of the authority of Jesus Christ, and the dishonor done to him by the nations, have set the children of Zion at variance among themselves; and all attempts to unite the churches in the present state of things will be in vain. While the cause continues the effect will remain. But let all christians of every name unite in advocating the claims of their Lord and King to universal empire, and the duty of the people to submit to him, and they will find themselves drawn more closely together, grounds of difference passing away, mutual criminations to cease, the bonds of a common brotherhood strengthened, and the ground prepared for a happy and permanent union of all the true friends of the Redeemer. Let all cease to justify the hostility of civil governments to their common Lord, and they will become reconciled to one another. Let the governments be reformed, and the churches will be united.

The adoption of this principle by all civil governments will be the cause of innumerable blessings to the world. The manifold evils that now afflict all nations will be removed or mitigated, impending judgments obviated, and the threatenings of divine wrath turned away. Under the reign and law of the Prince of Peace the nations will enjoy universal peace. Then they shall beat their swords into plowshares and their spears into pruning hooks: nation shall not lift up the sword against nation, neither shall there be war any more. All men shall be blessed in him, and all nations shall call him blessed. And blessed be his glorious name forever; and let the whole earth be filled with his glory. Amen, and amen.

"There is a tide (crisis) in the affairs of men, which taken at the flood leads on to fortune." The present is such a crisis with this nation. The signs of the times are ominous. The day of repentance to ungodly systems will soon be past. God is coming out of his place to punish the inhabitants of the earth for their iniquity; and the earth shall disclose her blood and no more cover her slain. Long has the prayer of all saints ascended to heaven: Pour out thy wrath upon the heathen that have not known thee, and upon the kingdoms that have not called upon thy name. (Ps. 79 : 6.)

The Lord Jesus Christ will soon take to himself his great power and reign. He will assert his rights and vindicate his character as the Governor of the nations. He shall speak to them in his wrath, and vex them in his sore displeasure. The present war is one of the strokes of his iron rod upon this nation. If this judgment does not humble the nation, and turn it to him that smiteth, He will visit it yet seven times more for its sins. Greater and more terrible calamities will follow, until either the government repents, or is destroyed.

Jesus Christ, the King of nations, is now entering upon his grand triumphant march through the nations, with his bow and his crown—the insignia of universal dominion, and of certain destruction to all who oppose it. He will strike through kings in the day of his wrath; he will judge among the heathen; he will fill the places with dead bodies; he will wound the heads over many countries. (Ps. 110 : 5, 6.) All who will not bow to his sceptre, shall be broken to pieces by his rod of iron. They that dwell in the wilderness shall bow to him, and his enemies shall lick the dust. Yea, all kings shall fall down before him; all nations shall serve him. (Ps. 72.)

I have not forgotten, my friends, that many and apparently insuperable obstacles lie in the way of the accomplishment of this work. This is to be expected. All great reformations have met with violent opposition. The Devil, who has always claimed the kingdoms of this world as his rightful possession, knowing the vast injury that would result to his kingdom if the Government of the United States should become Christian, will rally all the powers of earth and hell to oppose this movement. All the enemies of the Lord and his Anointed will arrange themselves in the line of battle against you; and most nominal christians, and many weak christians, discouraged because of their great and imposing numbers, will fall into their ranks. None but christians who have "a backbone," and are willing "to stand up for Jesus," can be counted upon as helpers in this work.

But let us not faint, nor turn back in the day of battle: there be more with us than with them. With them is an arm of flesh; but with us is the Lord our God to help us, and to fight our battles. The Lord of Hosts is with us, the God of Jacob is our refuge. There is no restraint with the Lord to save by many or by few. Be not discouraged or dismayed because of this great multitude; for the battle is not yours, but God's. Under the command of the Captain of the Lord's hosts, you have nothing to fear. He goes forth conquering and to conquer. The glorious titles, KING OF KINGS, AND LORD OF LORDS, written upon his vesture and upon his thigh, fill the ranks of his enemies with dismay and alarm, and inspire the hearts of his followers with courage and hope and joy. They are sure of victory—they are called and chosen and faithful. They are conquerors and more than conquerors—one shall chase a thousand, and two shall put ten thousand to flight.

I advocate no narrow sectarian tenet, but a great moral principle—as broad as the Universe and as high as the throne of God, and one which shall yet bless the world with righteousness and peace. It is the basis of millenial happiness! It is the great sheet-anchor of the hope of the Church and the world! It is alike the bond of brotherhood and the ground of joy of all christians on earth and saints in heaven! The worthiness of the Lamb to receive the service and homage of all creatures in the Universe is the grand theme of the song of the countless myriads of holy angels and redeemed men around the throne of God in heaven, and fills the high realms of glory and immortality with unceasing and everlasting hallelujahs!